T0285781

Graded Repertoire
for Guitar
Book Two

Stanley Yates Series

WWW.MELBAY.COM

Contents by Composer (1) easier (2) more challenging

Foreword

An important consideration in choosing material to study or teach is avoiding unnecessary technical or musical hurdles; although sometimes *idealistic*, a seamless technical and musical development in which motivating yet realistic goals are easily met is preferred. There is also much to be said for the control a student experiences when playing music that is below his or her current technical level, especially in performance situations. With this in mind, some overlap of difficulty has been incorporated between successive volumes in this repertoire series, within a carefully gauged increase in the overall difficulty level between volumes.

While the first volume in this series concentrates on pieces in open position with minimal left-hand activity, the technical focus of this second volume is an increased use of slurs and partial barres (of short duration) and an increased use of the second and fifth positions. Additional technical elements in-clude short trills, the occasional full barre, position changes, simple rasgueado, a continuation of arpeggio studies (including a short tremolo study), and an increased emphasis on modest scale textures and similar passagework. A didactic index may be found on page 85.

The pieces are grouped according to style period:

- early/traditional
- nineteenth century
- contemporary

Each stylistic division presents a (modest) range of difficulty levels, marked (1) or (2), and students should work from each of the three stylistic sections simultaneously rather than playing through the collection from cover to cover.

Technical Issues

Fingerings

It has not been felt necessary to indicate fingerings in this volume in as much detail as in the first, especially for the right hand; obviously, the fingering systems described in the accompanying text to the previous volume still apply, though the player should by now be capable of applying them unaided. The right-hand fingerings that do appear here signal unusual situations or act as an aid to reading through the music, and should spur the player on to determining appropriate fingerings where *automatic fingering* is inadequate. Similarly, indications for preparation and sequential placement of the left-hand fingers, found throughout the first volume, are now kept to a minimum.

Slurs

This volume makes frequent use of left-hand slurs and, in addition to simple ascending and descending slurs, includes compound slurs and short trills. Repeating the advice given in volume one, successful slur technique is determined almost entirely by hand position, along with the realization that a descending slur requires nothing more energetic than a simple plucking action with the left-hand finger in question.

Barres

Many pieces in this volume employ a partial barre (occasionally, a full barre). These are indicated by a position numeral and a superscript number designating the number of strings to be covered. In order to facilitate movement to the next required position, the number of strings covered by a barre may be greater than is needed to merely produce the notes at that point:

Damping

As mentioned in volume one, careful attention should be paid to silencing (damping) unwanted sounds, especially in the bass. Common situations that require damping with the right-hand thumb:

- to prevent an open bass string from continuing to ring beyond its written value (usually, the thumb returns to damp the note immediately *after* playing the next bass-note)
- to silence a bass note that is followed by a rest (the thumb plays and damps)
- in playing staccato notes (again, the thumb plays and damps).

Dynamics

Pay careful attention to the written dynamics and other expression markings! These markings are essential to the musical effect of the piece. Also bear in mind that written expression marks are only a starting point; individual players should augment them according to their own musical feeling.

No editorial dynamics have been added to the pieces in renaissance and baroque style, and none are contained in the original sources of these pieces. Nevertheless, players may still employ dynamics in these pieces (for example, by playing repeated sections loudly the first time, softly the second).

Practicing

- practice at a tempo that allows you to think ahead
- focus on one aspect of the piece at a time (for example, right-hand fingering, left-hand fingering, dynamics, tone quality, etc.)
- isolate difficult spots and practice them separately (and slowly)
- don't repeat the same mistakes over and over!
- practice without the guitar, looking at the score, and in your imagination

Metronome Markings

The metronome markings, provided for all of the pieces in this volume, should be regarded as suggestions only.

Stanley Yates

The Composers

Dionisio AGUADO (1784–1849)
A Spanish guitarist who associated closely with his fellow Spanish guitarist Fernando Sor in Paris. Aguado is best known today for his guitar method, the most detailed account of guitar technique of the time.

Mir ALI
A Pakistani-American guitarist who specializes in both classical and flamenco guitar styles.

Johann Sebastian BACH (1685–1750)
A German organist and church musician considered by many to be the finest composer who ever lived.

Carlo CALVI (fl. 1646)
An Italian guitarist who published a collection of pieces for the five-course Baroque guitar.

Matteo CARCASSI (1792–1853)
An Italian guitarist who worked mainly in Paris, one of the second wave of Italian guitarists to move there. His style is a little more romantic than that of Carulli, whose career was eclipsed by Carcassi. Both his guitar method, op. 16 and his 25 studies, op. 60 have remained in use to the present day.

Turlough CAROLAN (1670–1738)
A blind Irish harp player who made his living traveling from house to house, composing tunes for his prospective hosts along the way. He was the last great figure in the Irish harp tradition, and his surviving melodies were written down and published by his son, soon after his death. His surname is often (incorrectly) given as "O'Carolan."

Ferdinando CARULLI (1770–1841)
An Italian guitarist who spent most of his career in Paris, being perhaps the principal guitarist of the city before the arrival of Sor and, later, his fellow Italian Carcassi. Carulli was the most prolific guitar composer of the time (probably of any time!), his works reaching well over 300 opus numbers, many of which contained dozens of individual pieces.

Francis CUTTING (fl. 1600)
One of the finest lutenists of the English Renaissance about whom, apart from pieces of his contained in various lute collections of the time, almost nothing is known.

John DOWLAND (1563–1626)
A composer, singer, and probably the finest of the English lutenists. He traveled widely, was employed at various royal courts, and was known throughout Europe.

Georg FUHRMAN (fl. 1600)
A German lutenist and publisher, who published an important anthology of lute music, *Testudo-gallo-germanica*.

Gerald GARCIA
A British guitarist and composer, born in Singapore, and an Oxford-educated chemist!

Mauro GIULIANI (1780–1829)
An Italian guitarist who worked mainly in Vienna, where he was among the most celebrated instrumental performers of the time. He was personally associated with such illustrious musical figures as Beethoven, Rossini and Paganini, and took part in the first performance of Beethoven's *Seventh Symphony* (probably as a cellist).

Mark HOUGHTON
An English guitarist and composer who writes in a wide range of classical guitar styles.

Roger HUDSON
An American composer and guitarist whose music combines classical and popular influences.

Nikita KOSHKIN
A Russian guitarist and composer whose music has been performed and recorded by many leading performers, including himself. His best-known pieces include *The Prince's Toys* and the *Usher Waltz*.

Joseph KUFFNER (1776–1856)
An Austrian guitarist and violinist, court and military musician. He composed prolifically in all musical genres, including symphonic music, chamber music and opera.

Johann Kaspar MERTZ (1806–1556)
A Bratislavan (Czech) guitarist who traveled widely through Eastern Europe as a virtuoso performer on eight and ten-string guitars.

Santiago de MURCIA (fl. 1714–1732)
Spanish court guitarist who likely emigrated to the New World. His tablature collection for the five-course guitar *Passacalles y obras* (together with its recently discovered companion volume, the *Saldivar Codex*) is probably the single most important guitar collection of the Baroque period.

Antonio NAVA (1775–1828)
An Italian guitarist who worked mainly in Milan. Though virtually none of his music is available today, his method was one of the most successful Italian guitar publications of its time.

Stepan RAK
An innovative Czech guitarist and composer, whose music often draws upon visual imagery. Among his best-known pieces are *Elegy, Czech Fairy Tales* and *Voces de Profundis*—a piece inspired by the Alfred Hitchcock movie *Psycho*!

Lucas de RIBAYEZ (fl. 1680–1700)
A Spanish guitarist about whom little is known beyond his book of guitar music, *Luz y norte musicale* (most of which was taken from an earlier book by Gaspar Sanz).

Douglas SETH
An American guitarist and composer who has specialized in repertoire for younger students.

Ernest SHAND (1868–1924)
An English guitarist, famous during his lifetime as an actor. A collection of his guitar works, otherwise out of print for almost a hundred years, has recently been republished by Mel Bay Publications in the *Stanley Yates Series*.

Fernando SOR (1778–1839)
A Spanish guitarist and composer who worked mainly in Paris and London. Widely regarded as the finest guitar composer of his time, he also composed orchestral music, opera, and ballet. In addition to several extended concert works, he is well known to guitarists today for his sets of attractive studies.

Milan TESAŘ
A Czech guitarist and composer who has written several collections of pieces that combine classical guitar technique with popular musical idioms.

Robert de VISÉE (1650–c. 1732)
The finest French guitarist and lutenist of his time, employed at the court of the "Sun King," Louis XIX.

Stanley YATES
Yours truly! (see the back cover).

Andrew YORK
An American guitarist and composer whose music has been recorded by many leading performers, including himself.

Jaime Mirtenbaum ZENAMON
A Brazilian guitarist and composer whose numerous works include several sets of character pieces for students.

Terminology

Fingerings and guitar terms and symbols

1, 2, 3, 4 — fingers of the left (fretting) hand, index, middle, ring and little, respectively

(2) — alternative left-hand fingering

i, m, a, p — fingers of the right (plucking) hand, index, middle, ring and thumb, respectively

Circled numbers indicate strings

II³ — barre (in this case at the second fret covering the first 3 strings)

a dash (-) indicates that a finger remains on the same string, either at the same fret or at a new one

vib.	vibrato, pull the string back and forth	
bend	pull or push the string out of tune (sharp)	
har.	(natural) harmonic	
art. har.	artificial harmonic	
pont.	*ponticello* - pluck close to the bridge	
dolce	"sweet" - pluck over the soundhole	
ord	"ordinary" - pluck in the normal place	

left-hand slur

optional slur or editorial slur (not present in original source)

draws attention to a finger movement

"roll" - arpeggiate the chord (from the lowest note to the highest)

harmonics

rasg. ↑↓	*rasgueado* - strumming (up or down)
tambora, golpe	percussion, tapping on the bridge or guitar top
rs	rest-stroke (finger comes to rest on next string)
l.v.	*lasciare vibrare* - let the notes ring over one another
campanela	"little bells" - similar effect to l.v.

Musical terminology

Largo	slow		*lunga*	long, a long time
Adagio	slow		*grazioso*	gracefully
Lento	slow		*cantabile*	singing
Andante	walking pace - between slow and moderate		*pesante*	heavy
			marcato	marked
Andantino	on the slow side of moderate		*sostenuto*	sustained
Moderato	a normal, comfortable tempo		*espress.*	*espressivo*, expressively
Allegretto	on the lively side of moderato		*legato*	smoothly connected
Allegro	lively, fast		D. C.	*da capo* - go back to the beginning
Vivo	lively, fast		*Fine*	finish, the end
Tempo ad lib	you choose the tempo		*Coda*	the ending section of a piece
a tempo	return to the former tempo			
Meno mosso	a little slower		⌢•	fermata, pause or hold as long as you like
rit.	slower		'	short pause or breath
rall.	slow down gradually			
rubato	out of strict time		⌁ or *tr*	trill
ritmico	rhythmically			
pp	*pianissimo*, very soft		◁	like *crescendo*, gradually louder
p	*piano*, soft		▷	like *diminuendo*, gradually softer
mp	*mezzo piano*, a little bit soft			
mf	*mezzo forte*, a bit loud, normal volume			
f	*forte*, loud		**Articulation Symbols**	
ff	*fortissimo*, very loud			
sf or *fz*	*sforzando*, play this one note louder		>	accent, play this note louder
cresc.	*crescendo*, get progressively louder			
dim.	*diminuendo*, get progressively softer		•	*staccato*, this note should be cut short
poco	a little bit			
meno	less		—	*tenuto*, this note sounds for its full value (and a little bit more)
molto	a lot			
più	more		⌢	over-ring, this note continues to ring beyond its written value
sempre	always			
subito	immediately			
sim.	*simile*, the same			

Anon
(England, c.1600)

A Toye

This piece, a simple light-hearted "toye" to be "played with," comes from an English collection of teaching pieces for the lute signed and dated "Jane Pickeringe, 1616."

From the *Jane Pickering Lute Book* (England, c.1616).

Anon.
(England, c.1600)

Volt

From the *Dowland Manuscript* (England, 1600).

The volt (or volta) was a popular court dance and is found often in renaissance music collections. The dance consisted of a series of jumps and turns and was unusual for its time in that partners were allowed to actually hold each other - something that resulted in the dance being banned from the French court by Louis VIII!

Anon.
(England, c.1600)

The Sick Tune

A solo lute piece based on a popular song about the plague, "Sicke, sicke and very sicke!"

From Cambridge University ms D15 (England, 1600).

Anon.
(England, c.1600)

(2)

Kemp's Jig

Lively [♩ = c. 132]

m. 9:

In 1559, William Kemp, a famous comic actor and dancer, danced one hundred miles from London to Norwich to win a bet .

From the *Folger Lute Book* (England, 1600).

Anon.
(England, c.1600)

Wilson's Wilde

m. 2 and elsewhere:

This popular ballad tune was also known as "Wolsey's Wild" (after Cardinal Wolsey, the powerful advisor to England's King Henry VIII).

From the *Folger Dowland Manuscript* (England, c. 1600).

John DOWLAND
(1563-1626)

Orlando Sleepeth

Dowland named this piece after "Orlando Furioso," poet Ariosto's
epic and humorous account of courtly love and chivalry.

Cambridge ms D2 (England, c. 1600).

Francis CUTTING
(c.1600)

Packington's Pound

A setting for lute of one of the most famous Elizabethan ballad tunes, "Packington's Compound." The apparently handsome Sir John Packington made a bet (a "compound") that he could swim the Thames River from Westminster to Greenwich, but was prevented from doing so by his most powerful admirer, Queen Elizabeth I!

William Barley, *A New Booke of Tabliture for the Lute* (England, 1596).

Georg FUHRMAN
(c.1600)

Tanz (Dance)

The repeated "drone" accompaniment of this piece resembles a bagpipe or hurdy-gurdy, and gives the music a rustic feel.

From *Testudo Gallo-Germanico* (Germany, 1615).

Carlo CALVI
(1646)

[Baroque]

(1)

Tordiglione

An Italian version of the French "tourdion" — a light, fast dance.

From *Intavolatura di chitarra e chitarriglia* (Bolgna, 1646).

Lucas *de* RIBAYEZ
(*c. 1680*)

4 Dances from Baroque Spain

1 - CANARIOS

(2)

2 - GALLARDAS

From *Luz y norte musicale* (Madrid, 1677).

[Nos. 3 and 4 may be played together as a single piece, in the same tempo as follows: Paradetas-Rugero-Paradetas.]

vib. — quick, pronounced vibrato!

Slonflon

Lively [♩. = c.108]

D. C.

↑ — strum lightly in the direction of the arrow with <u>ami</u> together (or with <u>i</u> alone)

A typical Baroque guitar piece in "mixed" (strummed and plucked) style.
The meaning of the title, "Slonflon," is uncertain.

Chord diagrams from Gaspar Sanz' *Instrucción de música sobre la guitarra española* (1674):

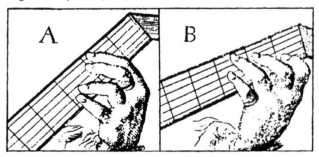

From an anonymous French guitar tablature, c. 1680.

Santiago de MURCIA

(c.1732)

La tia y la sobrina

An example of the popular *contredance* ("country dance") settings of English melodies that became fashionable in France and Spain around 1700.

The *campanela* passage in mm. 10-11 is a typical Baroque guitar effect that imitates the sound of "little bells."

Original tablature of the dance transcribed above:

From the *Saldivar Codex* (Spain/Mexico, c. 1732).

Robert de VISÉE
(c.1650-c.1732)

[Baroque]

(1)

Menuet

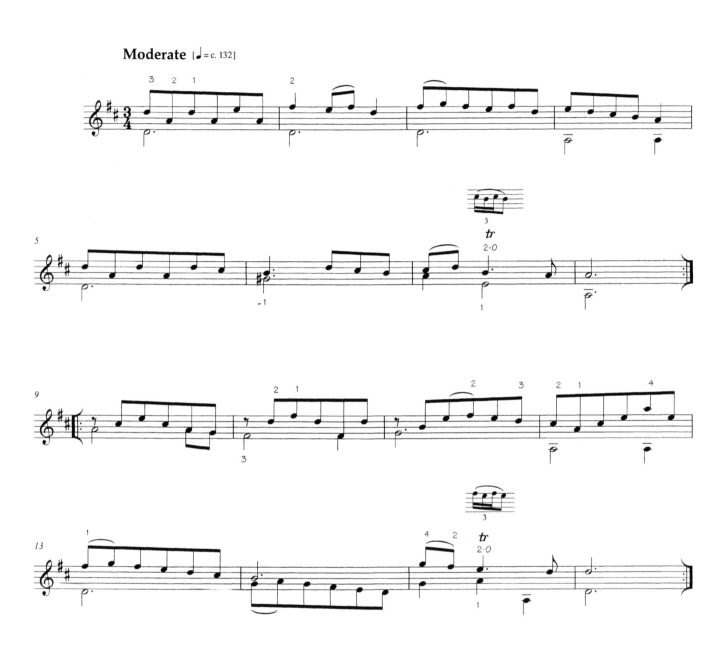

Menuet ("Minuet") — the most "dignified" of the Baroque court dances, often danced by the royal couple at the conclusion of the evening.

From an anonymous French manuscript c. 1680.

Johann Sebastian BACH
(1685-1750)

2 Pieces from the Anna Magdalena Notebook

1 - Minuet in G

Moderately fast [♩ = c. 132]

J. S. Bach was probably the greatest composer who ever lived. These two pieces are taken from a book of teaching pieces for the keyboard written by Bach for his wife, Anna Magdalena.

From *Clavierbüchlein für Anna Magdalena Bach* (Cöthen, c. 1725).

2- Musette in C (Bach)

Musette — a rustic French dance which suggests the drone of the bagpipes or hurdy-gurdy.

From *Clavierbüchlein für Anna Magdalena Bach* (Cöthen, c. 1725).

Turlough CAROLAN
(1670-1738)

[Baroque / Traditional]

(1)

Sheebeg an Sheemore (Irish Harp Piece, c. 1700)

Moderately slow [♩ = c. 112]

Harmonized by Stanley Yates

This piece depicts an ancient battle between two fairy kings that legend tells us took place in Ireland in the valley between two (actual) hills, Sheebeg and Sheemore.

Long (dotted) slurs, though enhancing the lyrical quality of the melody, are optional.

m. 23:

From *A Favourite Collection of Old Irish Tunes* (Dublin, c. 1780).

Turlough CAROLAN
(1670-1738)

Ode To Whiskey (Irish Harp Piece, c. 1700)

Harmonized by Stanley Yates

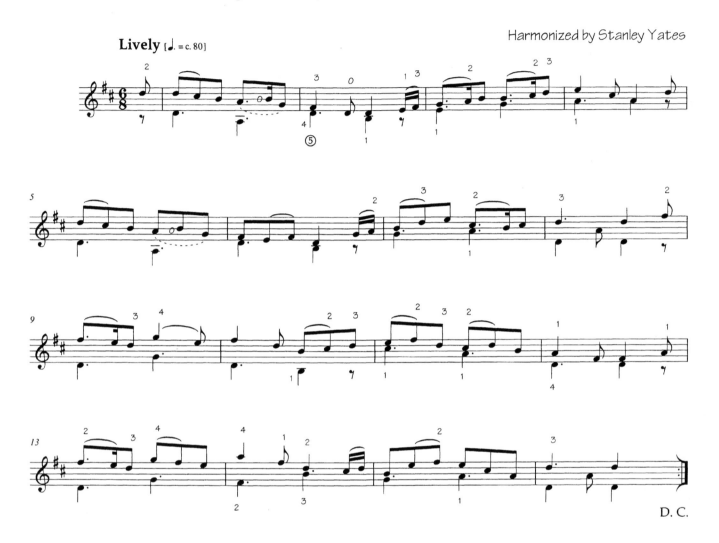

D. C.

This piece is a setting in double-jig rhythm by Carolan of his poem, "Ode to Whiskey:"

O Whiskey, heart of my soul!

You always knock me down.
I'm without sense, I don't know where I am!
You'd think that I'd take the warning.

My coat is all torn up and
I lost my cravat because of you.
But let all you've done be forgiven,
So long as you meet me again tomorrow!

Carolan's dying words, reputedly, were as follows:

"The drink and I have been friends for so long, it would be a pity for me to leave without one last kiss."

From *A Favourite Collection of Old Irish Tunes* (Dublin, c. 1780).

Anon-Traditional
(1700)

The Greenland Whale Fishery

(British-American whaling ballad)

Arranged by Roger Hudson

Deck the Halls

(1)

SY

God Rest Ye Merry Gentlemen

SY

Antonio NAVA
(1775-1828)

(1)

Allemande (Study in A)

Repeated-Note (Tremolo) Study in a-minor

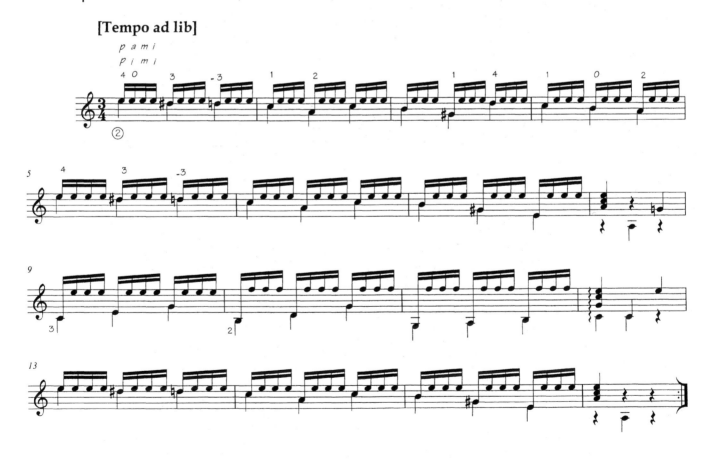

From *Metodo per Chitarra* (Milan, 1812).

Dionisio AGUADO
(1784-1849)

Study in a-minor

From *Nuevo Método* (Madrid, 1843).

Dionisio AGUADO
(1784-1849)

Arpeggio Study in a-minor

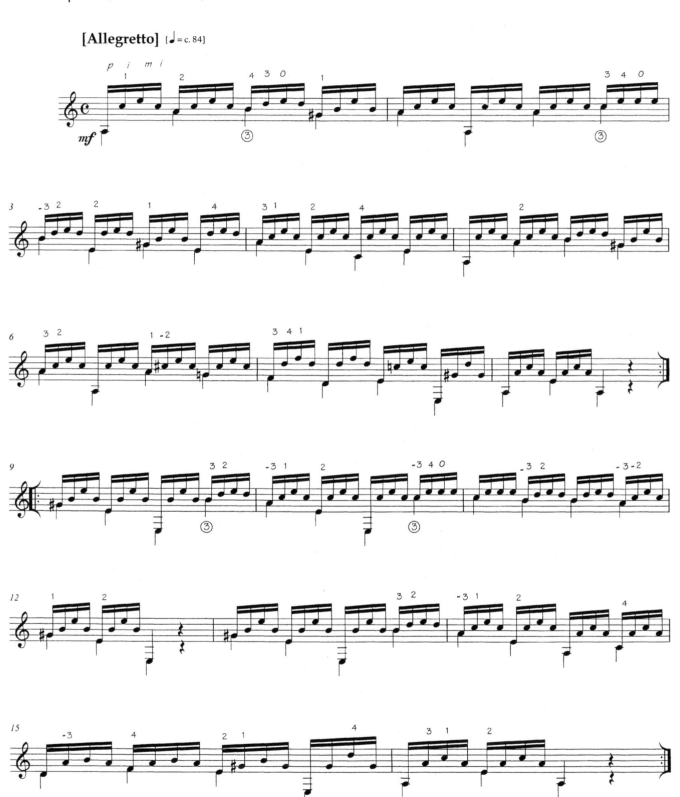

From *Nuevo Método* (Madrid, 1843).

Joseph KUFFNER
(1776-1856)

Cossaca (op. 80, no. 22)

(2)

Isolate the short scales in such places as m3 and practice them alternately slow and fast.

From *25 Leichte Sonatinas, op. 80* (Mainz, c. 1837).

Matteo CARCASSI
(1792-1853)

3 Arpeggio Studies (from op. 59)

No. 1 - Study in e-minor

Allow the first string notes to ring over, bringing out the melody.

The hinge-barre in m.13 is needed for strings three, four and five only.

From *Méthode complète pour la guitare, op. 59* (Paris, c. 1840).

No. 2 - Caprice in d-minor

From *Méthode complète pour la guitare, op. 59* (Paris, c. 1840).

No. 3 - Study in e-minor

(1)

Allow the first-string notes to ring over, bringing out the melody.

From *Méthode complète pour la guitare, op. 59* (Paris, c. 1840).

Matteo CARCASSI
(1792-1853)

Moderato in C (from op. 59)

From *Méthode complète pour la guitare, op. 59* (Paris, c. 1840).

mm. 49 & 52: "cross-fingering" - third finger stays
in place as the second finger slides beneath it.

Andantino Grazioso in A (from op. 59)

From *Méthode complète pour la guitare, op. 59* (Paris, c. 1840).

Mauro GIULIANI
(1780-1829)

Andantino in e-minor (op. 51, no. 5)

Aim for three distinct tone qualities in this piece:
bass (strong), treble (strong) and middle (lighter).

From *18 Lessons Progressive pour la Guitarre*, op. 51 (Vienna, 1814).

Mauro GIULIANI
(1780-1829)

Andantino in C (op. 139, no. 1)

m.19: cross-fingering — finger 1 stays in place
as finger 2 plays at the first fret on string 6.

From 24 *Prime Lezioni Progressive per Chitarra, op. 139* (Milan, 1840).

Ferdinando CARULLI
(1770-1841)

Larghetto in e-mi (from op. 241)

1

From Method complete pour la guitarre, op. 241 (Paris, c. 1825).

Ferdinando CARULLI
(1770-1841)

Moderato in b-minor (from op. 192)

(2)

From *La première année d'étude de guitare*, Op. 192 (Paris, c. 1811).

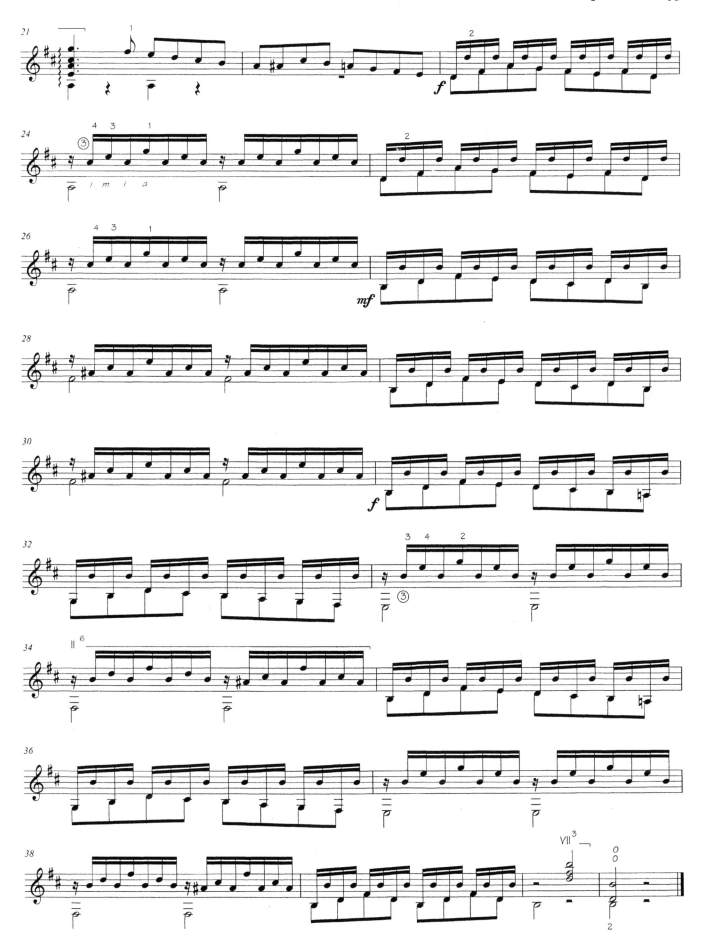

41

Ferdinando CARULLI
(1770-1841)

3 Preludes (arpeggios studies) from op. 114

1 - Prelude in E-major

(1)

[Tempo ad lib]

From *L'utile et l'agreable, op. 114* (Paris, c. 1817)

2 - Prelude in a-minor (op. 114 no. 7) (Carulli) (2)

[Allegro / Tempo ad lib]

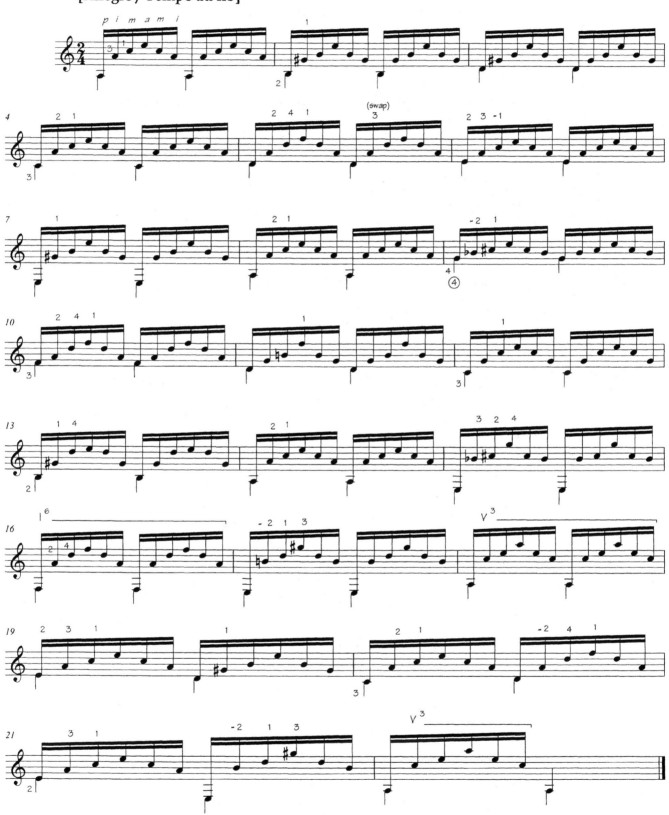

From *L'utile et l'agreable, op. 114* (Paris, c. 1817)

3 - Prelude in G-major (op. 114 no. 9) (Carulli)

[Allegretto / Tempo ad lib]

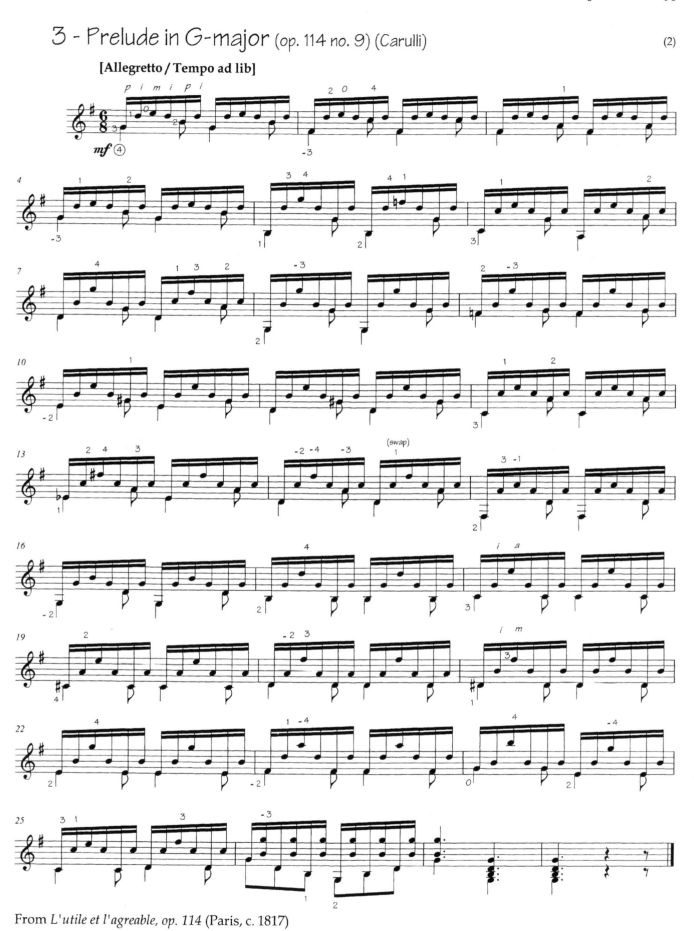

From *L'utile et l'agreable, op. 114* (Paris, c. 1817)

Ferdinando CARULLI
(1770-1841)

Siciliana in a-minor (from op. 241)

(1)

From *Method complete pour la guitarre, op. 241* (Paris, c. 1825).

Ferdinando CARULLI
(1770-1841)

Rondo in G (from op. 27)

(1)

Poco allegretto [♩ = c. 72]

From *Méthode complète por guitare, op. 27* (Paris, c. 1811).

Ferdinando CARULLI
(1770-1841)

Larghetto in e-minor (from op. 192)

(2)

From *La première année d'étude de guitare, Op. 192* (Paris, c. 1811).

Ferdinando CARULLI
(1770-1841)

Allegro agitato in d-minor (from op. 192)

(2)

From *La première année d'étude de guitare*, Op. 192 (Paris, c. 1811).

51

Fernando SOR
(1778-1839)

Moderato in C, op. 44 no. 6

(2)

From *Vingt-Quatre Petites Pieces, op. 44* (Paris, c. 1831).

Fernando SOR
(1778-1839)

Andante in b-minor, op. 31 no. 4

Andante [♩ = c. 60]

From *Vingt-Quatre Leçons Progressives, op. 31* (Paris, c. 1828).

Fernando SOR
(1778-1839)

Study in e-minor, op. 31 no. 6

(1)

[Andante] [♩ = c. 108]

From *Vingt-Quatre Leçons Progressives, op. 31* (Paris, c. 1828).

Fernando SOR
(1778-1839)

Andante in a-minor, op. 35 no. 14

(1)

From *Vingt-Quatre Exercises, op. 35* (Paris, c. 1828).

Fernando SOR
(1778-1839)

Cantabile in d-minor, op. 44, no. 17

(2)

From *Vingt-Quatre Petites Pieces, op. 44* (Paris, c. 1831).

Johann Kaspar MERTZ
(1806-1856)

(1)

Moderato

Moderato [♩ = c. 88]

From *Schule für die Guitare* (Vienna, c. 1847).

Johann Kaspar MERTZ
(1806-1856)

Nocturne

(2)

From *Trois Nocturnes,* Op. 4 (Vienna, c. 1840).

Ernest SHAND
(1868-1924)

Study in e-minor (from op. 100)

With each change of left-hand position, set the hand for as many notes as possible.

From *Improved Method for Guitar, op. 100* (London, 1896).

Ernest SHAND
(1868-1924)

Valse in G-major (from op. 100)

(1)

From *Improved Method for Guitar*, op. 100 (London, 1896).

Ernest SHAND
(1868-1924)

[19th Century]

(1)

Valse in A-major (from op. 100)

m. 16: prepare the barre as finger 2 frets the G#.

From *Improved Method for Guitar, op. 100* (London, 1896).

Ernest SHAND
(1868-1924)

Lento (from op. 100)

(2)

From *Improved Method for Guitar, op. 100* (London, 1896).

Ernest SHAND
(1868-1924)

Gavotte (from op. 100)

From *Improved Method for Guitar, op. 100* (London, 1896).

Roger HUDSON

Ancestral Bells

(2)

Andrew YORK

Sherry's Waltz (from *8 Discernments*)

(1)

[Allegretto] [♩ = c. 144]

Mir ALI

Flamenco Suite

1. Farruca

Allegro [♩= c. 116]

rs - *p* plays rest stroke and remains on the string during the *i* finger rasgueados (except m.13).

2. Solea

Allegro [♩ = c. 96]

golpe: tap on lower part of soundboard with <u>*am*</u> together
rs: rest-stroke (finger rests on next string after playing)

3. Tangos

(1)

4. Allegrias

Allegro [♩ = c. 116]

5. Rumba por Givi

INTRO (rubato) [♩ = c. 116]

(2)

Tempo de rumba [♩ = c. 116]

(rs) = rest-stroke

70

Jaime Mirtenbaum ZENAMON

Romance (no. 14 from 20 *Epigrammes*)

(1)

[Moderato] [♩ = c. 104]

Practice the rhythm by counting "1 & 2 & 3 & 4 &," gradually replacing the "2," "3" and "4" with a whisper.

Jaime Mirtenbaum ZENAMON

La luna y el sol -"The Moon and the Sun" (no. 16 from 20 Epigrammes)

(2)

Milan TESAŘ

Ballad (no. 10 from *20 Jazz Images*)

(1)

Nikita KOSHKIN

[Contemporary]

Le pélerin - "The Pilgrim" (no. 1 from *Suite "six cordes"*)

(2)

Moderato [♩= c. 92]

m. 21: play the first-string F with a temporary full barre at the first fret (to avoid cutting short the low F on the sixth string)

Douglas SETH

Myron's Storm

Moderately fast [♩ = c.126]

Stepan RAK

[Contemporary]

The Old Castle (no. 11 from *15 Descriptive Pieces*)

(2)

Gerald GARCIA

Amour Soucoupier (no. 1 from *25 Etudes Esquisses*)

(2)

Marcato [♩ = c.132]

Mark HOUGHTON

Passacaglia

Mark HOUGHTON

Duke's Tune (after Duke Ellington)

(2)

Stanley YATES

Polka

(1)

Moderately fast ("Tempo di Sagreras") ♩ = c.104

From *En Mode - 22 Easy Character Pieces for Guitar*.
© 2001 Stanley Yates, Mel Bay Publications, Inc.
Used by Permission.

Stanley YATES

Etude mécanique No. 5

From *Etudes mécaniques - 12 Easy–Intermediate Studies for Guitar.*
© 2001 Stanley Yates, Mel Bay Publications, Inc.
Used by Permission.

Stanley YATES

E-Jam Blues

Didactic Index

New Didactic Works by Stanley Yates

En Mode - 22 Easy Character Pieces for Guitar (MB20008)

1 - Prelude

2 - Valse Russe

3 - Folksong

4 - Old Dance

5 - Musette

6 - Koto

7 - Taiko

8 - Jasmine

9 - Prelude

10 - Allemande

11 - Sarabande

12 - Gavotta

13 - Giga

14 - Villanella

15 - Tango antigua

16 - Polka

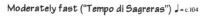

17 - Malaguenesque

18 - Processional

19 - Mode Bulgaro

20 - Amazonia

21 - Tango nuevo

22 - Short Blues

Etudes mécaniques - 12 Easy-Intermediate Studies for Guitar (MB20007)

No. 1

No. 2

No. 3

No. 4

No. 5

No. 6

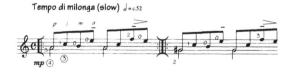

No. 7

No. 8

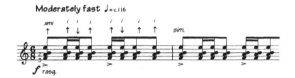

No. 9

No. 10

No. 11

No. 12